Fjords Travel Guide

Sightseeing, Hotel, Restaurant & Shopping Highlights

Emily Sutton

Copyright © 2014, Astute Press
All Rights Reserved.

No part of this publication may be reproduced, stored in a retrieval system, or transmitted, in any form or by any means without the prior written permission of the publisher, nor be otherwise circulated in any form of binding or cover other than that in which it is published and without similar condition being imposed on the subsequent purchaser.

If there are any errors or omissions in copyright acknowledgements the publisher will be pleased to insert the appropriate acknowledgement in any subsequent printing of this publication.

Although we have taken all reasonable care in researching this book we make no warranty about the accuracy or completeness of its content and disclaim all liability arising from its use

Table of Contents

Norwegian Fjords 5
   Culture 6
   Location & Orientation 7
   Climate & When to Visit 8

Sightseeing Highlights 10
   Ryfylke District 10
   Sunnhordland District 12
   Sognefjord 13
   Hardangerfjord 15
   Stavanger Region 16
   Flåm Village 17
   Sunnfjord 18
   FjordKysten 19
   Trondheimsfjord 20
   Nordfjord 21
   Voss Village 22
   Bergen 23

Recommendations for the Budget Traveller 25
   Places to Stay 25
      Centrum Romutleie 25
      Montana Family & Youth Hostel 26
      Skansen Pensjonat 27
      Park Hotel Vossevangen 27
      Midtnes Pensjonat 28
   Places to Eat & Drink 28
      Wesselstuen 28
      Jacobs Bar & Kjøkken 29
      Sjøhuset Skagen 30
      Årestova 30
      Sjøbua Fish Restaurant 31
   Places to Shop 31
      Norsk Flid Husfliden 31
      Bryggen Husflid 32
      Audhild Viken 33
      Kvadrat Shopping Center 33

Saga Souvenir 34

Norwegian Fjords

The world famous Norwegian Fjords are located in west Norway near to the cities of Bergen and Ålesund. They were recently rated as the world's top tourist destination by the esteemed National Geographic magazine. Geiranger, in Møre og Romsdal and Nærøyfjord, in Sogn og Fjordane are also highly-rated UNESCO World Heritage sites.

The scenic nature is completely different from what you could ever imagine, even if you have seen hundreds of photos of the region. It is no wonder National Geographic Magazine named this "the world's most iconic destination."

You should make an effort to visit here at least once during your lifetime to experience its majestic and untouched nature.

This part of Norway is home to some of the world's largest coral reefs. Also, the fjords represent the most fertile fishing ground in the world. Expect to see a lot of photographers wherever you go, as it is one of their favorite places to do their work. It is not unusual that they picked Norwegian Fjords, since you there are a lot of mountains, waterfalls, glaciers and more at every turn. It takes a trip like this one to realize how powerful nature is.

The local currency in Norway is the Norwegian Krona (NOK), and it is equivalent to $0.17, €0.13, or £0.11.

Culture

Much like the nature, the people are very pleasant. You won't have a problem with language, since almost everyone can speak English, while in bigger villages and towns you will meet a lot of people who can also speak German and French. The culture itself is pretty mixed in all of the regions of West Norway.

This is the place where you will see the true definition of teamwork. Even if the people don't know each other, they know that they form a community, and will help out each other with whatever. They also feel obligated to protect this region, which is a beautiful thing. When you hear the music of their orchestras you will certainly feel the true magic of Norwegian Fjords, as they add that unique touch to the preserved nature. Their paintings of the fjord landscapes are just as delightful as the actual place. Much like they care for the nature, they also do for their culture and local traditions.

There is no type of stereotype here. People are individuals, and you will see that when talking to the first two or three people you meet. They have a great balance of being up to date with the world's trends, while still keeping their local roots.

Location & Orientation

Norwegian Fjords are located in West Norway. Just in case you don't know, a fjord is a long, narrow, deep inlet of the sea between high cliffs, typically formed by submergence of a glaciated valley. There are also numerous waterfalls in this region, and many of them fall directly into the fjords.

The roads are an attraction themselves. It doesn't matter if you go by car or by train; you will surely keep your eye stuck to the window (unless you are driving). However, getting around by car is more recommended, since you can make stops to enjoy the view whenever you want, and you will also have a chance to go to more places. Some destinations are best to go by boat, and you will be offered with this type of transportation no matter what village or town you are in. It too shows you the unique beauty of the fjords, in its own way.

You are bound to find countless small villages at every turn. Some bigger towns are somewhat rare, but you will get to them with no problem. The great thing is that locals are so in love with the nature around them, so they will almost always go on a hike with you just so they can get you to the attraction or village you planned on visiting.

Climate & When to Visit

The climate in this part of Norway isn't that cold, considering its altitude, because of the influence of the Gulf Stream. It is tough to know when you should visit, because it depends on what you like to experience. We can only say that there is no bad time to visit the Norwegian Fjords. However, keep in mind that most people choose to visit during summer. If we could recommend a period of time it would be either spring or autumn, because we think that those seasons really bring out the best in the preserved nature of the fjords.

For the current weather in Norway see:
http://www.holiday-weather.com/country/norway/

July is the peak of the summer, when you shouldn't be surprised if temperatures reach 25°C or more. It is a popular month in this region due to long, sunny days. September is also quite a popular month, because of the colors of the fjords. You should definitely see how the yellow nature and sun rays collide, creating a unique gold color. In the winter you will enter a paradise for skiers. People who love this sport will definitely have to visit during December. However, this is the period when rainfall is quite frequent and heavy. For some, spring is the most satisfying season for visiting, more specifically, the month May. You will see the fjords blossom and turn green.

Sightseeing Highlights

Ryfylke District

If you are coming from the south, then Ryfylke will be the first thing you'll encounter, and one of the most divine on your trip. This is where the Lysefjord (probably the most popular fjord in the world) lies, where you can find mountain formations of Preikestolen (Pulpit Rock), of which you have certainly seen several photos, due to its enormous popularity. The Pulpit Rock offers you a great panoramic view. Be prepared to spend at least two hours there, as we guarantee that the beauty will hold you there.

Another mountain formation called Kjerag is a place that you should definitely visit. There is a popular path to the plateau, from which you will have a rewarding view. You definitely won't know how to explain to anyone else what it feels like to look at a fjord from the height of 1.1 kilometers. But, the view and the feeling you get while looking will certainly be stuck in your mind forever. Over the last couple of years, it has become extremely popular to take a picture on Kjeragbolten, a round rock stuck in the mountain crevice. Beside from the view, the adrenaline rush you get while walking on the paths of this mountain also adds an irreplaceable feeling. We wouldn't advise people who are afraid of heights to go on this journey. Both of these formations are also very popular for base jumpers.

Other than hiking, we also suggest you take at least one boat trip from Ryfylke, in order to visit the fjords of this region, from a different viewpoint. Many boats will take you really close up to some stunning waterfalls, and that is also a thing that you can rarely experience. Aside from what we already mentioned, you must visit Sandsfossen Waterfall, and we know you will be tempted to do this, since you will be able to hear it all year round.

If you are interested in the culture and history of this place, then we suggest you visit the prehistoric village Landa. You should also try the local salmon, and if you are the adventurous type, then you should eat the one you catch. There will always be a local or two that will gladly take you fishing.

Sunnhordland District

There are plenty of things to do in this district that is located at the mouth of Hardangerfjord. It is a place many come to relax a day or two. You have a great view of the ocean, and once you sit down you will keep staring for a couple of hours, at least. It is a great place to spend the afternoon or morning with a sandwich and a drink.

After you are done relaxing your mind, it is time for some activity. You must take a walk to "Norway's roof." Otherwise known as the Folgefonna, it is Norway's third largest glacier. And if you have never been to one before then you absolutely must go. It is your chance to walk on snow that never melts, and to enter small caves and passages made completely out of ice. Don't worry about any kind of danger; it is the safest glacier in Norway. Even if you are familiar with what will await you, it is always fun to go on an expedition like this. If you want to fully experience what Folgefonna offers, then you should go with trained glacier guides, as you will even climb crevasses together with them.

While in the area of Sunnhordland, don't miss your chance to visit Langfoss. It is often cited as one of the world's most beautiful waterfalls. However, you will see a few other less popular waterfalls in the area. Just like Ryfylke, this district is great for fishing. The rivers are some of the best in the world for catching salmon. If you still have spare time, then you can't go wrong with hiking on the many paths and mountains Sunnhordland offers.

Sognefjord

This area is located in the middle of Norwegian Fjords, and is the longest fjord in Norway (the second largest in the world) at the length of 205 kilometers. It is also the deepest fjord in the world. It is one of the most popular areas, because of the numerous activities that are available. Let's start with The Jostedalsbreen National Park – the largest glacier in mainland Europe. That is just the beginning of the whole journey on Sognefjord. You should also visit Jotunheimen National Park, where you can see beautiful and untouched mountains, including the highest ones in Norway. Not only that, but it is also the place where the highest mountain pass in Northern Europe is.

Other than the nature there are also cultural significances situated here like Urnes Stave Church; the oldest church in Norway, from the first half of the 12th century. Afterwards, head on to Fjaerland, a village located in the municipality of Sogndal. Here you will have a chance to go both to the Glacier Museum (there are interactive exhibitions, along with many videos of glaciers displayed) and Book Town.

One of the most recommended things to do is to go to an unforgettable journey with Flåm Railway. It is one of the most scenic and breathtaking stretches of railway in the whole world. It will take you from the mountain station Mydral through the steep and narrow Flåm Valley, to the Flåm Village. Note that this is one of the world's steepest railways. This is a 20 kilometer long journey, and you will have a chance to go the height of 865 meters by train. After you have taken this journey, we recommend you visit the Railway Museum & Documentation Center that is free of charge. Of course, you shouldn't only go by train. Take a boat tour, or hike to some of the most beautiful waterfalls in Norway. This is the area that is home to Vettisfossen – Norway's highest protected waterfall. Other notable mentions include Feigumfossen, Kjosfossen and Kvinafossen.

The most popular activity is hiking, since you will be properly rewarded by the extraordinary views for every step you take. However, you can also take part in kayaking, rafting, horse riding, summer skiing and mountaineering.

Hardangerfjord

This is a place extremely popular for its trekking spots, along with beautiful plants that grow in the area. It is the third largest fjord in the world, and the second largest in Norway, at the length of 179 kilometers. It is quite popular thing to look at magnificent panoramas and sunsets. During spring it gets really beautiful, due to fruit trees blossoming. And you will without a doubt see both kids and older people standing by the roads selling delicious fruit. You must try some of their local fruit specialties. Keep in mind that about 40% of fruit in the whole Norway is grown in this area. It is home to a few small towns, and is a bit more touched by settlements than other places of the Norwegian Fjords.

There are a few museums that you should consider visiting, if you want to learn more about the culture, history and art of the people. You will find a wide array of topics displayed in them. The first one that you should visit is Hardanger Folkemuseum, which is an open-air museum that showcases national costumes and Hardanger fiddles. The next stop for you should be Agatunet – a farm cluster dating back to the Middle Ages. And the last one we recommend is Kunsthuset Kabuso og Ingebright Vik Museum, an art museum with a variety of exhibitions, from Norwegian Romanticism to international contemporary art.

This area offers the usual fjord activities such as fishing, hunting, cycling, kayaking, glacier walking, hiking and skiing. We suggest you visit the great falls of this area, along with the glaciers. Also, be on the lookout for Hardangervidda. Getting to the vast mountain plateau (one of the largest in Europe) of it is a must.

Apart from those activities we recommend that you visit one of the fruit farms in villages like Lofthus and Ulvik. These are little places that have survived for hundreds of years, thanks to the amazing fruit. Expect to see a lot of cherries, apples, pears and plums, and of course, try them out. It is also highly recommended for you to try out either their cider, or apple juice. It is without a doubt like none you have tried before.

Stavanger Region

This region is sure to remain in your memory forever. There is just so much nature to experience and the greatest thing about it is that it is within easy reach. It doesn't matter what you want to visit. Mountains, rivers, fjords and beautiful sandy beaches are all close to you. Boat trips in this region are a must! Trust our word, you won't regret it.

It is a region with a great cultural scene. It seems to have it everything when it comes to nature too. Whatever your interests are, you are bound to find something for you. Whether it is history based, museums, magnificent Nordic architecture or lively festivals. It is no wonder that Stavanger region was picked as the European Capital of Culture in 2008.

The citizens of Norway love to come to this region because of the uniquely prepared food. When you try it out, you will be hooked on it also, and will definitely want to come back here just for another plate. Stavanger is also the region that organizes Gladmat, the biggest food festivals in the Nordic countries. The festival takes place at the end of July, and has over 250,000 visitors annually.

While hiking, you should go on the path that will take you to Manafossen Waterfall, which has a free fall of 92 meters, making it the biggest waterfall in this county. Apart from that, you should really visit Solastranden beach, which you will often see in lists of the most beautiful beaches in the world. It is the longest sandy beach in the whole Norway. It is a wonderful thing to go skiing one day, and surfing the next, and the Norwegian Fjords offer that. After you are done with beach-like activities, you should also consider visiting some of the lighthouses by the coast.

Flåm Village

This village is located in the innermost part of Sognefjord. It is easily accessible by any method of transportation. You can come here by taking an unforgettable trip on the Flåm Railway that we mentioned in the Sognefjord section. It is famous both for the activities it offers, as well as the cultural scene in the village. The first thing that you absolutely must do is go to Otternes Bygdetun that offers 27 different buildings, some even from the 1600's.

It is has local cultural significance and is considered a "living museum." After that, you should spend half an hour watching the film "Living with the fjord." You can see the film whenever you want, since it is shown every day of the year. You will see it in the cinema Flåm Panorama any time from 11 am to 7 pm. The cinema can house only 75 people, but you will almost always find room to sit down and enjoy the film.

You can take a trip to the nearby Undredal where you will be able to try their delicious blue and white cheese. While you are there, we would also advise you to check out Undredal Stave Church, which is from 1147. It is the smallest stave church in the whole Norway.

The famous Kjosfossen Waterfall is located in the Flåm area. It is definitely a stop that you must take, especially if you are a photography enthusiast. It is advised that you go on an expedition to Aurlandsfjord and Nærøyfjord, as they represent some of the world's most scenic places. Nærøyfjord is known as the narrowest fjord in the world and is a part of the UNESCO World Heritage List. Other than the stunning untouched nature, you will also be viewing wildlife and old settlements in the high mountain areas. If you want to explore in a bit more lively way, then we suggest you go kayaking, as it presents a whole different experience.

Sunnfjord

When you come here, you will definitely get the feeling that this area is alive; everything from the slow-moving rivers to powerful waterfalls will convince you of this.

Expect to see waterfalls everywhere (a total of 50). No wonder it is called Fosseheimen (Waterfall Country). It is not that hard to get to most of them. In fact, there is a trail that is more than 21 kilometers long following the watercourse. This is the most popular trekking path, called Waterfall Trail. You will see 14 large waterfalls when walking on this trail. There are four waterfalls that you absolutely shouldn't miss out on – Likholefossen, Vallstadfossen, Huldefossen and Eikjelandsfossen. There is a great trail that leads from Sunnfjord Museum to Huldefossen.

However, that is not the only superb thing about this place. It is also home to Jostedal Glacier, the largest one in Mainland Europe (100 kilometers long). The glacier has countless arms reaching into valleys in Nordfjord and Sogn. One thing that you should also do is take a ferry to Norway's westernmost active fishing island community, Bulandet.

Sunnfjord is a real cultural treasure, and offers a lot in both art and history. The main museum of the area is Sunnfjord Museum, which offers interesting exhibitions about the history and culture of the region. You will even get a chance to see some buildings where people lived during the 1500's. There is one more museum that we would recommend – The Black Friday Museum. It is dedicated to the day in February, 1945 when a great air battle in Norway took place over Sunnfjord.

FjordKysten

This is as west as you will go in Norway. The fjord coast is delightful all year round. However, summer is the most popular season to visit FjordKysten. The coastal walks then are just priceless. But, don't be fooled by that. If you come during any other period of time, you will still have a lot of things to do; like diving during wintertime, or sitting in a lighthouse watching a stormy night in October and November. During summer don't miss out on island hopping. That will certainly fill your journey with even more extraordinary natural beauty.

So after you are done sitting across the open sea, watching the waves splash; it is time to get up and visit everything else the coast of fjords has to offer. This area is very rich, culturally and historically. You will find many preserved historical monuments, as well as numerous areas from the Viking era. This was a very popular Viking region, due to the coast. Apart from all the monuments and buildings from that time, you can also feel what it is like to be a Viking by going to Dalsfjord and sailing along the fjord in a Viking ship. Of course, all tourists who know a thing or two about this area will go to millstonepark in Hyllestad, as it is full of unique geological features. You will also hear about this park from some locals. It is so famous because it has been nominated for the UNESCO World Heritage List.

Trondheimsfjord

This place is really popular due to its ice-free nature all year round. It is an astonishing marine life that holds over 90 species of fish. It is a really relaxing place where you should consider taking a day off from hiking and enjoying the nature around you. However, if you don't want to rest, then you can still have somewhat of an extreme adventure, as some braches of the fjord are hardly accessible and challenging. With a little more effort than usual, you will still reach you planned destination.

Trondheimsfjors is the third largest fjord in Norway, with the length of 130 kilometers. It is really popular during the summer due to the sunshine that really brings out the color of the fjord. It is also popular then because there are a lot of open lakes, and that is the season when water activities are popular.

It also became popular over the last couple of years because beautiful deep sea corals were discovered in the fjord. It is surrounded by many fishing towns where you can enjoy a nice meal and drink or simply spend the night.

Nordfjord

You can enjoy a lot of things in this place, from lively activities such as canoeing, rafting and summer skiing to visiting some interesting cultural and historical sites. Nordfjord is a place for people who really want to do a lot of things. Hiking is absolutely amazing here thanks to over 200 trails that will take you to mountain summits, farms and all types of landscape. If that is not enough action for you, then you can go glacier walking at the Jostedalsbreen National Park. It is sure to hit you with an adrenaline rush.

We also suggest you don't miss out on Skåla, Norway's longest uphill slope with the height of 1,848 meters. Other than the extreme fun and challenging climbs, you will also be rewarded with an immensely beautiful view of the fjords. Keep in mind to also visit the tower on top of Skåla, which is a really popular tourist spot. The next thing you should do is either go summer skiing of surfing. The conditions for surfing are perfect here, because of the big ocean tides and the white sandy beaches.

Remember that this place is also very interesting when it comes to cultural significance. There is one thing that is a must when it comes to historical heritage of this place, and that is Selje Monastery. The monastery is located on Selja Island. Both locals and tourists have been coming here for years, so they can see Norway's first pilgrimage site along with the rare relics from the Viking Age. You will probably hear the story of Sunniva who was a martyr on the island, but after his death pronounced a patron saint of West Norway.

Voss Village

Voss Village is a place full of excitement, and is visited by countless tourists, as well as Norwegians for this particular reason. One of the more popular activities in this area is to go on Stalheimskleiva Mountain Road, which is one of the steepest roads in Northern Europe. While on the road you can observe two divine waterfalls – Stalheimsfossen and Sivlefossen. Speaking of waterfalls, this area has one that is extremely popular. Tvindefossen is a waterfall that is 152 meters high. It is located next to Tvinde camping site. By following the road passing the camping site, you will reach the top of the Tvindefossen. Watch out, because the path is not fully secured.

Enough walking; if you want to relax a bit and still get to a great viewing point then you shouldn't be worried. Close to the village center you can hop in a cable car which will take you to the top of Hanguren Mountain. Once you reach the top, there will be a café waiting for you. Grab a drink and enjoy the panoramic view over the Voss village center, along with the beautiful landscape.

A great historical monument of this place is Vangskyrkja. It is a church built in the 13th century that is still in use to this day. Voss is great because it offers both great physical activities, as well as interesting cultural attractions. Apart from hiking, mountain biking and sky diving, you can also enjoy numerous festivals taking place in the village all year round.

Bergen

After all the small towns and villages, it is time to visit a city. However, this might not be the type of city you envisioned. It has its own uniqueness, because it is somewhat big, but still has that small town feel. The city is rich with festivals, as well as numerous outdoor activities such as golf, kayaking, rafting, paragliding and hang gliding. It is a place located on the UNESCO World Heritage List.

Bergen is constantly packed with tourists from all over the world. This shouldn't surprise you, since it holds the title of European City of Culture. The city has a highly developed cultural scene, and great museums that you should visit. Yes, strolling around Bergen is a very good idea, but don't forget that you also have a lot of great natural attractions in the area also. A popular thing to do is take a 7-minute ride on Fløibanen Funicular, which will take you to an amazing viewing point from which you can see the city center, mountains and fjords. There are also numerous paths waiting for you here, along with a nice café.

An interesting thing you can do is visit the Bergen Aquarium. You will have a chance to see a number of seals, penguins and more creatures that can be found below the surface of the sea. They also have a tropical section, which houses crocodiles, snakes and more. Another cool thing to visit, and somewhat of a new attraction, is Bergen Science Center. Here you can see around 100 experiments and devices used in the fields of natural science and technology.

Recommendations for the Budget Traveller

Places to Stay

Centrum Romutleie

Baldersgata 7, 4011 Stavanger, Tel: +47 97 96 67 57
http://www.centrumromutleie.com/#!english

You won't need much more than this guesthouse. It is located in Stavanger, and the rooms are clean and cozy.

There are only single and double rooms available. You have a kitchen that you can use. Internet is available also. Keep in mind that smoking is not allowed. A single room will set you back NOK 400, while a double will cost you NOK 500.

Montana Family & Youth Hostel

Johan Blytts vei 30
5096 Bergen
Tel: +47 55 20 80 70
http://www.montana.no/en

After a day filled with hiking and activities you will need a proper rest and the Montana Family & Youth Hostel is perfect for that.

The hostel is located in an astonishing surrounding up the hillside of Mount Ulriken, which is located about 5 km south of the city center of Bergen. They offer everything from a single room to an 18-bed dormitory. The price for a single room is NOK 475 – 650, while the double will cost you NOK 650 – 750; a room with 4 beds will set you back NOK 920 – 1180, depending on the season. Breakfast is included in the price.

Skansen Pensjonat

Vetrlidsallmenningen 29
5014 Bergen
Tel: +47 55 31 90 80
http://www.skansen-pensjonat.no/

Skansen Pensjonat is a really good choice. It is a small house located in the center of Bergen. It is great if you are looking for a quiet place where you can rest. Breakfast is included in the price, as well as Wi-Fi. While staying here you will also experience a great view overlooking the city. A single room will cost you NOK 450 - 500 (depending on the size), while the double will set you back NOK 800.

Park Hotel Vossevangen

Uttrågata 1-3
5700 Voss
Tel: +47 56 53 10 00
http://www.parkvoss.no/

This hotel is located in the center of Voss. All rooms in the hotel have their own private bathroom. A single room will set you back NOK 1,075, while the price of a double room is NOK 1,550. Breakfast is included in the price, along with Wi-Fi. In the complex of the hotel you will also find Pentagon Night Club, which is one of the most popular night spots in Voss.

Midtnes Pensjonat

Kong Belesveg 33
6898 Balestrand
Tel: +47 57 69 42 40
http://www.midtnes.no/

You will surely feel at home if you are staying in Midtnes Pensjonat. It is surrounded by beautiful nature, in the small village of Balestrand (located on the edge of Sognefjord). Trust us; there is nothing better than waking up here and getting to the balcony to enjoy the morning view. Private bathrooms are included in all of the rooms. A single room will cost you NOK 790; while a double room will set you back NOK 990. Breakfast is also included in the price.

Places to Eat & Drink

Wesselstuen

Øvre Ole Bulls plass 6
5012 Bergen
Tel: +47 55 55 49 49

This is Bergen's classy (yet cheap) restaurant that opened in 1957. It is one of the favorites among locals, due to its cultural importance for the city.

It gets quite romantic during the night, so if you want to tale a loved one out somewhere, this is definitely the place. A meal will set you back around NOK 300; we also suggest you try out some of their desserts, which will cost you an additional NOK 100. It is open from 11am to 0:30am every day except Sunday. On Sunday it is open from 2pm to 11:30pm.

Jacobs Bar & Kjøkken

Kong Oscars 44
5017 Bergen
Tel: +47 55 54 41 60
http://www.jacobsbergen.no/en/web/static/index/id/contact/

This Restaurant in located in the center of Bergen. Their main focus is on local ingredients. Their chefs are highly acclaimed across Europe, and have won several prestigious awards. You will have a chance to choose from a great selection of meat and seafood dishes. A meal will cost you around NOK 250, but if you want to really experience the food, then we suggest you order the 4 course set menu that will set you back NOK 595. It is open every day, except Sunday. The restaurant is open from 4pm to 10pm.

Sjøhuset Skagen

Skagenkaien 13
4006 Stavanger
Tel: +47 51 89 51 80
http://sjohusetskagen.no/en/

Sjøhuset Skagen is a part of a Stavanger property that was built before 1710. The house of the restaurant itself was built in 1770. Of course, it has changed a lot from its original form, but you can still feel the history of this house. They have a really great menu that offers both Norwegian and international culinary specialties. It is open every day. From 11:30am to 11pm from Monday through Saturday. On Sunday it is open from 1pm to 9:30pm.

Årestova

Nedkvitnesvegen 25
5710 Skulestadmo
Tel: +47 56 51 05 25

This is a really delightful restaurant located in Voss Village. It is built in the traditional style, which means that it looks like a Viking house. It has a great surrounding, as it is located by Lake Lundarvatnet. Their focus is on using as much local product as possible. The restaurant is even more beautiful during summer, since they add tables in front of the restaurant. Eating here and watching the lake is something that will surely calm your mind.

Sjøbua Fish Restaurant

Brunholmsgt. 1A
6004 Ålesund
Tel: +47 70 12 71 00
http://www.sjoebua.no/en-US/default.aspx

The restaurant is in an old wharf side warehouse in the town of Ålesund. This is one of the best seafood restaurants in the region. The food is, of course, made from fresh materials from the local area. When you get inside the restaurant you will see a bowl of live lobsters and shellfish, and you will be given the option to choose which lobster is going to be prepared for you. It is open on workdays only, from 4pm to 1am. However, keep in mind that the kitchen is open until 11pm.

Places to Shop

Norsk Flid Husfliden

Vågsallemenning 3
5014 Bergen
Tel: +47 55 54 47 40

This store was established in 1895 with the purpose of promoting Norwegian crafts, as they are a great reflection of their culture and traditions.

The store nowadays is occupied by tourists every day, who absolutely love all of the products that are sold, as they represent a great souvenir. The most popular items are Norwegian traditional jewelry and tableware. If you buy something here, it is sure to last long and to remind you of your trip. It is located in the city of Bergen.

Bryggen Husflid

Bryggen 19
5835 Bergen
Tel: +47 55 32 88 03
http://www.sweaterspecialist.com/

This shop is located in Bergen, in the old wooden houses at Bryggen, which is on the UNESCO World Heritage List. It is a family run business that specializes in woolen knitwear ever since 1989. They offer the largest collection of hand-knitted sweaters in the whole country, and are of top quality. However, these are still rare products. They are also immensely popular as gifts. You can choose from a wide variety of cardigans and pullovers for men, women and kids.

Audhild Viken

Bellgården – Bryggen
5003 Bergen
Tel: +47 55 21 54 89

Ever since Audhild Viken started producing woven products, back in 1947, the store has been growing more and more popular. It is greatly visited by both locals and tourists because of their top quality clothing designs. The shop is also popular among tourists, as they have a section dedicated to Bergen souvenirs, as well as Norwegian souvenirs.

Kvadrat Shopping Center

Gamle Stokkav. 1
4313 Sandnes
Tel: +47 51 96 00 00

After visiting the local shops find some time to spend a part of your day in a big shopping center. Kvadrat is the fourth largest shopping center in Norway, and has over 160 shops (and 14 restaurants) in its complex. It is located in Sandnes, in the Stavanger Region. It is the most visited attraction in the whole region. The shopping center is open from 10am to 8pm on workdays, and from 10am to 6pm on Saturdays. It is closed on Sundays.

Saga Souvenir

Pb. 54
5742 Flåm
Tel: +47 57 11 00 11
http://sagasouvenir.blogspot.com/

If you still haven't found the perfect souvenir from this part of Norway, then you should immediately head down to Flåm Village. There you will find a great shop that is located in the center of the village, and is one of the largest gift shops in the country. Clothes, art, toys, and everything else that you can think of can be found in this store.

Printed in Great Britain
by Amazon